Gunner

HURRICANE HORSE

BY JUDY ANDREKSON

Illustrations by David Parkins

Tundra Books

Text copyright © 2010 by Judy Andrekson
Illustrations copyright © 2010 by David Parkins

Published in Canada by Tundra Books,
a division of Random House of Canada Limited,
One Toronto Street, Suite 300, Toronto, Ontario M5C 2V6

Published in the United States by Tundra Books of Northern New York,
P.O. Box 1030, Plattsburgh, New York 12901

Library of Congress Control Number: 2009938092

Library and Archives Canada Cataloguing in Publication

Andrekson, Judy
Gunner : hurricane horse / Judy Andrekson ; illustrated by David Parkins.

(True horse stories)
ISBN 978-0-88776-905-4

1. Gunner (Horse)–Juvenile literature. 2. Show horses–United States–Biography–Juvenile literature. 3. American paint horse–United States–Biography–Juvenile literature. 4. Hurricane Katrina, 2005–Anecdotes–Juvenile literature.
I. Parkins, David II. Title. III. Series: True horse stories

SF295.187.G85A54 2010   j798.2'40929   C2009-905855-3

We acknowledge the financial support of the Government of Canada through the Book Publishing Industry Development Program (BPIDP) and that of the Government of Ontario through the Ontario Media Development Corporation's Ontario Book Initiative. We further acknowledge the support of the Canada Council for the Arts and the Ontario Arts Council for our publishing program.

Design: Terri Nimmo   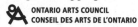 ONTARIO ARTS COUNCIL
CONSEIL DES ARTS DE L'ONTARIO

Printed and bound in Canada

5 6 7 8 9   20 19 18 17 16

Dedicated to my Nanny, Ina York.
I want to see the funny side of life forever,
just like you do.

Acknowledgments

Many thanks to everyone who so graciously shared their stories of this remarkable horse with me. Although this is a fairly simple story, it turned out to be one of the more difficult research projects I've taken on, mainly due to the tumultuous circumstances the Lott-Goodwin family has endured in the past few years. Heather, I am so grateful that you finally said yes, and that you stuck it out for the many weeks of endless questions. Gunner's story is very worth sharing, and I hope in some way it helps you to have it in book form.

Thanks also to the American Paint Horse Association for all the valuable information you have available about Paint horses and the major shows and with your assistance in locating the Lott-Goodwins. Maria Lott, thank you for sharing the story from your perspective. Heather is very lucky to have you on her side. Thanks to Brent Becknow and Mike Stable for adding your voices and memories of your experiences with Heather and Gunner. I have to say thanks, too, to Bryan Shoemaker, for your great sense of humor and for helping Mike navigate the "scary computer." Robert Owens, thank you so much for sharing your photos of Gunner. You helped make the book extra special.

A long overdue thank you goes out to David Parkins who has illustrated each of my books, and has done a wonderful job on this one. I've never met or spoken to you David, but you are a part of this writing journey of mine, and I am grateful for all you've done.

Finally, I would like to express my very deep gratitude to all of you at Tundra Books who have worked so hard at helping me realize the dream of seeing my stories in print. It's been an absolute pleasure working with you.

Contents

I

Unwanted

Heather Lott-Goodwin disliked the homely, potbellied runt of a colt from the first moment she watched it leap awkwardly off the trailer after it's mother. He was a golden chestnut with high, white stockings on all four legs and a bold, white face, but his hide was so coated with grunge that is was hard to tell where the brown stopped and the white began.

Heather sighed as she recognized yet another good-for-nothing horse. They'd be stuck with paying more for feed than it was worth, then not being able to sell it later. E.W. was always bringing home these misfits!

She scowled at her husband when he handed her the mare's lead rope so that he could unload the cow that had been included in the trade he had made with a local horse breeder. He had driven to J.C. Horses in Laurel, Mississippi, not far from their own ranch, that afternoon to make a deal on some haying equipment. The breeder was going out of business, and E.W. was always on the lookout for a good deal. It was the mare E.W. wanted. She was a nice, little American Paint with pretty markings and surprisingly good bloodlines – a nice addition to his broodmare band. She just happened to have this colt, and so he brought him home too.

While E.W. unloaded the cow, Heather had her hands full trying to keep the mare calm while the colt wandered and explored, instead of staying at her side the way any self-respecting baby would in a strange environment. This was obviously not a well-behaved son, though, and he soon had his mother frantically whinnying, twisting and turning at the end of the lead rope, trying to keep track of where he had gone.

Heather was so focused on calming the mare that

she didn't even notice the colt come up behind her, but he got her attention soon enough when he scampered in, bit her on the behind, and darted back. Heather let out a yell of pain and surprise and spun around find him standing just out of reach, head turned to watch her intently with his one fierce, blue eye. If she had disliked the look of him before, she now disliked his bratty personality even more and didn't trust him one bit. Rubbing her sore bottom, she was soon giving E.W. an earful about bringing home such unpleasant animals . . . again! And E.W. was laughing.

Life had changed drastically for that mischievous foal that afternoon, although he didn't know it yet. He had spent his first months at his dam's side in a small yard with several other farm animals, existing in mud and boredom. He had never been handled, although he was quite accustomed to humans and had no fear of them. He would approach people boldly enough, accept the scratches and rubs and occasional treats they supplied. To him, they were simply playthings.

No one had ever tried to halter him or train him in any way. Moreover, his playfulness had made his first owners a bit nervous of him; his naturally dominant, coltish behaviors had been unwittingly rewarded. A quick nip or kick could send those human "playmates" scurrying. This was normal horseplay, but didn't make for great horse-human relations. It was, however, end-lessly amusing to the bored youngster.

Being loaded onto the big, dark stock trailer was the first frightening experience in his young life, and it had taken a bit of herding and persuasion to get him to jump into the noisy box after his mother. He had huddled near her side when the door banged shut behind them, and had trembled violently when the engine roared to life, making the darkness move beneath his feet. But he soon became accustomed to the swaying and bumping of the trailer and, true to his nature, his fear had turned to mis-chievous curiosity by the time they had reached their destination.

Such an interesting place they had come to! He could smell other horses, and lots of other animals. Fields and forests stretched out as far as his eyes could see. This was a ranch of over two thousand acres, with more green, open space then he had ever seen. The spirited little soul was yearning to explore, but he soon realized that his dam was not able to follow. As adventurous as he was, he was still very young and looked to his mother for safety, and so he turned his attention on the "playmates" close at hand.

The human at his mother's head was interesting – a small, dark-haired woman with a strong voice and a feeling of "leader," which was something he'd never noticed in these humans before.

Surprisingly, she paid him little attention. She barely looked at him, and she didn't try to reach out and touch or scratch him like most of the other humans he had known. She didn't jump away as he approached her . . . in fact, she seemed to be ignoring him completely. His little stud-colt heart took this as a challenge, and he decided that this human needed to know who was top pony here.

Instead of running away when he sank his teeth into her, she spun and faced him, even taking a step toward him. For the first time in his young life, he didn't dare approach for another try. Her look told him that she, in fact, was the top pony around here, and he'd better not mess with her. Instinct told him to respect this, and he was too young to challenge it. He sniffed the air, gathering her scent, and watched her closely. He'd have to remember this one!

"Let's just put them in the paddock here for now," E.W. suggested, ignoring Heather's tirade about the colt.

"What on earth are we going to do with that sassy little thing?" Heather protested. "He looks like he's full of

worms. He should have shed that shaggy baby coat by now. And don't even get me started on his attitude . . ."

E.W. watched him quietly, as the colt explored the perimeter of the new paddock. If you looked past the grime and the wormy belly and the baby hair, there were fine, straight legs, a broad chest, a pretty head set on a well-formed, nicely arched neck, and intelligent, quick eyes. It was true, he did look a little worse for wear right now, but E.W. wasn't worried. He had the mare; the colt was not a big concern to him.

"The colt's old enough to be weaned. I think we'll let them settle, then get him ready to go out with the other weanlings right away. He'll make a decent little roping horse in a couple of years. He just needs good pasture and time to develop. He'll be nicer than you think."

Heather rolled her eyes. "I've heard that before," she mumbled, as she turned away from the paddock and walked to the house, rubbing her bruised rump as she went.

That evening, the mare was led to the barn, colt in tow, and into a roomy box stall, deeply bedded with sweet-smelling straw. E.W. quickly led the mare back out, and before the colt could follow, Heather closed the door. The mare was instantly upset, attempting to return to her young son, but E.W. coaxed her away from the barn and to a pasture as far from the area as he could take her.

Inside the barn, all hell had broken loose. At first the colt had simply stood, statue still, straining to hear his mother's voice. But as it faded and he could no longer see her, he became frantic, storming around the stall, charging the door, filling the barn with his desperate cries. It would be one of the longest and most miserable nights of his life, a night where snuggling close to his dam's side and nursing would have been the best thing to do, had she been there. He had never been alone. There was no mischief in him now. He was pure misery, and even Heather felt sorry for him.

His pitiful cries continued through the night. By morning his voice was hoarse and his pacing slowed by exhaustion. He welcomed the comforting touches of another creature when E.W. rubbed his neck and soothed him, and he drank deeply from the bucket of water in the kind man's hands. He showed little interest in his food, however, and after a short rest, was straining to see over the stall door again, searching for any sign of his mother.

He had quieted considerably by later that day, and E.W. decided he would be better off out with the other colts and fillies. The pasture he found himself in was wonderful, enough to spark even the most unhappy colt's interest. It was at least forty acres of rolling grasslands and forest just waiting to be explored. A band of unruly weanlings were already there, waiting for him to come play. E.W. had picked up several babies from a breeder in north Mississippi a few weeks earlier, and a couple more from a local auction. It was now late August 1999, and the colt was the last to join the herd. They would be left to grow for a year or so before being trained then either worked on the ranch, or resold.

Heather had very little to do with the colt in the year that followed, although every time their paths would cross, she was reminded of why she disliked him so much. If she went with E.W. to check on cows or put out feed for the young horses, the colt would always find ways to challenge and annoy her. She felt his teeth again one day at the feed trough. Given the chance, he'd splash her with water, or kick out at her as he ran past. With every incident, E.W. would get an earful about "that colt." All through that winter, E.W. heard a thousand reasons why they could do without a horse like him. The colt was odd looking, growing faster at one end than the other, unbalanced and bad tempered and . . . it went on and on.

E.W. was soon convinced that this was just the right

horse for his lively young wife to work with. He didn't tell her so yet, though. She was carrying their first baby that winter, and he was in no rush.

Heather had grown up on horseback and was a fearless, talented show rider. Her father, Morris Lott, had been a jockey, until a back injury forced him to turn in his silks and try his hand at show horses and judging. He had established a show stable in Diamond Head, Mississippi, and had raised his family, along with over two hundred horses, on his impressive property. He was a dedicated horseman and Heather had grown up with horses in her blood.

Heather's mother, Maria, had supported her husband's endeavors whole-heartedly, although she was not a horsewoman when they first met. She was soon heavily involved though, showing and caring for the animals and her family, as well as pursuing her own career in education.

Eventually, Morris and Maria had downsized, moving to a small farm in Picayune, Mississippi, to be closer to where Heather was attending school. Their stable was drastically reduced to just a handful of horses.

E.W. had also grown up with horses and farming, having taken over his grandfather's ranch while still in high school. It had been overgrown and run-down when he had moved there, but by the time he met Heather and convinced her to marry earlier that year, it was a productive, working ranch, and a place where they looked forward to raising a family of their own.

E.W. felt certain that Heather could not only manage this colt, but somehow *needed* to.

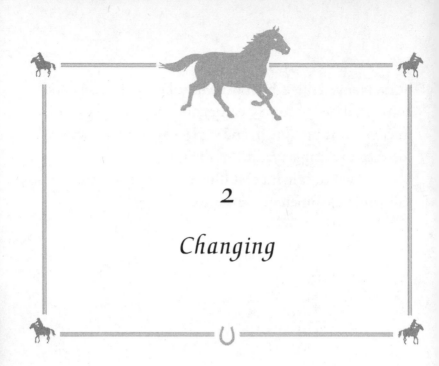

2

Changing

E.W. began training the youngsters from the yearling herd the following spring, starting with the oldest and most developed animals, and leaving the colt until last. He was still runty and needed time to grow. E.W. was just getting these babies started – asking little more than their acceptance of handling, the halter, bridle, saddle and a rider. They were too young to work yet, but he liked to put a foundation on them before they were much older. It was easier to sell them that way, or to work with them later.

Heather had developed problems with her pregnancy early that spring. This first baby of theirs was eager to be born, far too soon for safety. Heather was put on complete bed rest. Any excessive activity or excitement could cause her to go into premature labor. That's why she was not involved when the colt was pulled from the big pasture, and E.W. started to work with him.

She could not be left alone for any length of time, so her father started coming to stay with her during the day while E.W. worked. He kept her apprised of the progress being made with the young horses and the workings of the ranch and helped her cope with the restlessness that nearly drove her insane for the next month. When her father mentioned that E.W. had brought in a little Paint colt to start, Heather screwed up her face in disgust. "Waste of energy, that one," she predicted. "He shouldn't have brought him home in the first place."

A month later, Heather was allowed out of bed, but she remained housebound, allowed only as far as the front porch. From her seat on that porch, she had a full view of the paddock, the barns, and the round pen, where E.W. did most of his work with the young horses. Her father would sit beside her, calling out advice to his son-in-law as he worked with a particular horse. For Heather, this was infinitely better than being in bed.

When her birthday arrived, Heather was heavy, housebound, and a little cranky. E.W. kissed her that morning before heading out to care for the livestock, but did not leave her a gift, or suggest that one was coming. Throughout the day, not a word was mentioned about it being her birthday, and despite her greatest efforts to ignore this, by that afternoon, she was feeling hurt and upset that her husband could have forgotten.

That evening, E.W. asked her to come for a short truck ride to the barn to see something. She was not allowed to walk far, but could be driven for short distances. She reluctantly agreed.

E.W. parked outside the horse barn and turned to her with a playful smile. "Bet you thought I forgot your birthday, huh?"

She couldn't help but smile back, wondering what he had up his sleeve. "I was just about ready to tell you that you'd be sleeping on the couch tonight," she admitted.

"Well, I didn't forget," he said. "I was keeping this a surprise until just the right time." He held out an envelope, which she took from him eagerly.

Inside was a set of papers, and it took a moment before she realized what it meant. They were registration papers for a new horse . . . a sorrel overo Paint colt. Her eyes were excited when she looked up at E.W. again. He grinned and said, "Thought you could use a project to look forward to. Wait here."

When E.W. came out of the barn, leading her new colt, Heather's excitement turned to disbelief and anger in an instant. At the end of the lead rope was the shaggy-coated, disproportioned, ugly colt that she'd been complaining about all winter. He couldn't possibly be serious. *This* was her birthday present?

That night, E.W. slept on the couch!

For the rest of that month, Heather watched from the porch as E.W. started working with "her" colt, teaching him basic verbal commands on the lunge line in the round pen, handling him until he became accustomed to having his feet and body touched all over.

The colt was not as passive and ready to submit to new things as some of the other youngsters had been, and he was a real challenge for E.W. He fought the halter, preferring to go his own way. He shied at E.W.'s touch. He bucked at the feel of the saddlecloth on his back. He was spirited and stubborn and, being a natural herd leader, he was used to having things his own way. He didn't like the idea of giving in to these humans who used to be so easy to intimidate.

E.W., in his quiet way, brought him around, patiently but firmly, and although the colt continued to be mischievous and, at times difficult, he was learning his lessons well. When E.W. wasn't annoyed with him, he was impressed by him. This was a smart colt, probably one of the nicest he had started that summer. And he knew that his wife, set as she was against him, was seeing the very same thing.

Often, when the colt was in his paddock and Heather was in her chair on the porch, the young horse would come to the fence, sniff the air, and just stand and watch her with that one blue eye.

One day, annoyed, she stomped a foot at him and shouted, "What are you looking at?"

Startled, he leaped back from the fence a few feet, then came right back with a deep whinny, as though answering her challenge.

She waved a hand at him. "Scat!"

He circled and returned to the fence, shaking his head, striking with his front hooves, and whinnying again. It was the first "conversation" they had, the first of many to follow in the weeks to come. It became a game that kept them both amused and occupied during long hours of confinement – and the beginning of a very special relationship.

There were days when Heather was confined to her bed again, and on those days E.W. would complain about how destructive and obnoxious the colt could be. He almost seemed to be missing her and letting the world know all about it. When Heather would return to her chair on the porch and their little game could commence, the colt became cooperative again.

As the weeks passed, the yearling began to develop muscle from the daily work in the round pen, and his body changed from awkward adolescent to graceful youth. Heather began to notice the smoothness of his trot, the arch of his neck, and his pretty head. With daily handling and grooming, he finally lost his long baby hair. In its place was a coat that shone with striking markings that were really quite attractive.

"You know, you may just be able to turn a profit on that colt after all," she said to E.W. one day.

E.W. grinned at her and answered, "I think that's one of the first nice things you've said about him. And you named him too. Profit. Perfect name!"

Heather made a face at her husband and retorted, "Yeah, well I didn't say I like him. I'm just saying we might be able to sell him, and thank goodness for that!"

With the coming of August, Heather's confinement was over. Although she was restricted by her size and discomfort, at least she could walk the grounds and visit the goats and dogs and horses.

She could watch up close as E.W. worked with Profit. She could touch him, groom him, and get to know him better. She liked what she found. He had settled well under E.W.'s guidance and was proving to be an affectionate and likeable little horse, even though he often gave them some reason to curse him. He could untie knots, escape secure fences, and would eat everything in sight, including your lunch if you left it where he could reach it. He was constantly getting into trouble, but he was not mean, and Heather started to really enjoy him.

One day, Heather begged E.W. to let her work with Profit in the round pen, just for a few minutes, just to get the feel of him. E.W. was reluctant, but Heather was persuasive, and he finally agreed and brought the colt out to her. Profit was going well in the round pen now, responding calmly and consistently to voice commands such as walk, trot, lope, whoa, back, and reverse. E.W. watched them get started, then, feeling secure about his wife's safety and ability, he headed back to the barn to do some other work, instructing her to call him when she was finished.

Heather was in her glory. It had been months since she had stood at the center of the round pen, watching a young horse move around her. Months since she had been able to move with another animal and connect mentally and physically. She had missed it!

Suddenly, Profit stopped moving and planted himself in front of her, facing the outside fence. "Hey, what are you . . . ?" Then she spotted it. E.W. kept a small herd of goats, and coming right toward her was the biggest, meanest billy she'd ever seen, with his head lowered and his great, curved horns obviously ready for the charge. She called out to E.W., but he didn't hear her. Profit came between them, shaking his head at the bad-tempered creature and warning him to stay away. Again and again, the goat tried to charge her, head down and to one side in a butting position, but Profit cut him off every time. Finally, E.W. heard Heather's cries and ran out with one of the farm dogs to help her. He was amazed to find Profit working the goat like a cow horse, head down, front legs splayed, charging and backing off and doing his best to keep Heather safe.

The next day, the goat disappeared forever, and Heather went into labor, delivering their baby boy. They named him Wesley William, and Profit was raised to hero status.

3

Show Horse

In the months to follow, Heather and E.W. were extraordinarily busy with the new baby, the running of the ranch, and Heather's eventual return to work as an emergency room nurse at Touro Hospital in New Orleans. Heather's father was now having health problems, and Heather found herself returning the favor he had given her, spending time with him while her mother worked at her job as principal of a school in Picayune.

E.W. continued training Profit, progressing now to basic work under saddle. Heather was more than eager to get back into the saddle. When time allowed, she would assist E.W., taking her place aboard the head-strong colt. Profit bucked when the spirit moved him, shied at every opportunity, and acted like the immature teenager that he still was. But between pranks and acting up, he was learning the ways of a saddle horse, and the foundation training they gave him in those months would take him a long way in the years to come.

The more Heather worked with him and got to know him, the more she liked him. He still had growing up to do, and he could still make her angrier than any horse on the place, but he was slowly working his way into her heart. He reminded her of another horse she had loved and lost, the first horse she had called her own and became seriously competitive on.

Ebony Winsalot was the reject of her father's stable, a bad-tempered, large black mare with a blaze running the length of her face. Heather rode all of the horses in her father's stable, but Ebony became a favorite and, for several years, she was Heather's mount of choice. The spirited pair had been a regular sight on the Gulf Coast show circuit, and Ebony was Heather's first Superior All Round Horse, a title she coveted and hoped to earn again one day. Now, as she felt Profit moving out beneath her, long and smooth, responding to her lightest touch, as the bond between them began to develop, she wondered if she had been given more of a gift then she had realized.

The name on Profit's registration papers was PBJ Decks Smokin Gun, a name that honored one of the greatest-ever Paint horses, Colonels Smokin Gun. Heather started calling him Gunner, which was easier to say than that son-of-a-gun. As soon as E.W. heard her starting to use the nickname on him, he knew that this little horse would not be sold and would be making them no profit at all!

Like his parents, baby Wesley was destined for a life with horses. They bought him his first pony, a little buckskin gelding named Buttermilk, when he turned six months old, and he spent as much time in the stable with Mom or Dad as he did in his nursery. He was able to sit a horse almost before he could walk, and most of his early childhood adventures involved a horse.

Buttermilk became Gunner's favorite companion, and the pair was nearly inseparable. Gunner threw a fit every time Buttermilk was out of his sight. He spent that winter growing into an elegant two-year-old, but mentally he was still very much a baby. Buttermilk was young enough to be a playful and entertaining companion, but old enough to be a calming influence and a teacher when the need arose. Gunner was always more settled when the pony was close by.

As Gunner approached his second birthday, Heather was setting her sights on getting back into the show ring. She knew she wouldn't have time to put the finishing training on Gunner that he'd need in order to start his career, however. She simply couldn't fit it in with her work at the hospital and the demands of a baby. She decided to contact a trainer from Texas who had worked with several of her father's horses and was well respected in the show scene.

Mike Stable had a reputation for bringing out the best in young horses without burning them out by asking too much too soon. The horses he started would still be in the show ring years later, not breaking down mentally or physically, as so many young horses would under the pressure to perform. Mike's specialty was the all round horse, or a horse that could work on the ranch, roping and cutting cattle, then take it's owner for a safe and mannerly trail ride, be used in pony club by the kids on the weekends, and have beautiful manners when handled from the ground. In short, it could do anything it was put to, in either English or Western style, and be able to do it well. The all round horse needed to be versatile, athletic, and well trained. The American Paint

Horse Association, like many other breed associations, liked to offer classes and awards to show off the versatility and superiority of the breed.

This was Heather's passion as well, and it was the Superior All Round Paint Horse title that she would be chasing in the coming years on Gunner.

Gunner was far from an all round horse when Mike first started working with him. He was a green-broke baby with a good solid foundation, but little more. He was still far more interested in playing then he was in working, and he was constantly trying Mike's incredible patience with his antics. But he was a fast learner . . . and even though he often got into trouble, Mike loved his personality and his willingness to learn. Most of all, he admired the young horse's natural athleticism – an essential quality in the all round horse. Within a short time of starting with him, Mike was convinced that they would go far with Gunner.

Mike was as certain of Heather's talent as he was of Gunner's. He had watched her grow up on her father's horses and knew she could ride anything with fur and four legs and make it look easy. She was fearless and bold and was able to impart that same confidence to her mounts. He also knew that she would put in the time to give her horse its best shot. So many of his clients would send him a horse to have it trained and prepared for a show, and then ride it for the first time in months just minutes before the class. They'd then complain to Mike, wondering why they didn't do as well as they'd hoped. Mike and Heather shared a similar motto – if you want to drive a car, go buy a car. A horse was a living, breathing, unpredictable creature . . . and even a talented trainer like Mike couldn't turn a horse into a car.

Although they were in different states, Mike and Heather were in close communication in the coming months about Gunner's training. Mike was putting more polish on his basic walk, trot, lope, and reverse, working toward quick response times, smooth transitions, and a soft, balanced way of moving. As the colt developed muscle and skill, Mike began adding lead changes, low jumps, obstacle work, and showmanship handling to the colt's training. Later they would ask for more, but Gunner was still just a youngster, and Mike didn't want to put a damper on the colt's spirit or hurt him physically, so he kept it fairly simple that first year.

By the time Heather flew out to work with them early in 2002, Gunner was a different horse. He had grown, now standing just over fifteen hands high, and his body was muscular and lithe. Mike had him in peak condition and groomed to perfection when she arrived.

Heather could hardly believe that this was the scruffy brat that had given her so much grief not so long ago. Mike was quick to assure her that there was still plenty of brat in him, but they were both excited about the show year ahead, and Heather couldn't wait to try Gunner out.

Heather took him home for a while that spring and started him at a few small, local shows, to give him exposure to the show atmosphere and to help them get to know each other again. He did well in the Hunter Under Saddle classes that year, having a natural, long, smooth trot and nice style over small jumps. This would be one of his strongest classes in the years to come, as his natural abilities and way of moving served him well in this work, but he was soon proving that he could hold his own in just about any class.

At home, Gunner reminded his owners that he was still that same mischievous, troublemaking colt that they had known. It seemed that they were constantly getting him out of scrapes, catching him when he had escaped, finding things that he had destroyed, or patching him up when he tried to destroy himself. Heather and E.W. agreed that they had never met such a curious and annoying colt, but the very personality that had once caused Heather to dislike him so much, now made her love Gunner all the more.

The following winter, Gunner again returned to Texas, this time with the plan to start his show career in earnest. He was almost three and looking better than any of them had expected. His body had balanced out and muscled up and no longer seemed out of proportion. The potbellied, shaggy baby of the past was now a gleaming, handsome show horse.

Heather was competitive and took her career seriously. She was excited to have a horse that challenged her abilities and had the talent to go the distance. But, she also had a full-time job, a baby, and family demands to juggle, so she had to choose a path that would suit her situation and still give Gunner the chance he deserved.

She could keep him home and continue attending the smaller shows in their region. The competition wouldn't be as tough and he'd do well there, but it would mean that she'd have to do most of his training, and they'd be on the road almost every weekend, both of which required the one thing she didn't have enough of . . . time.

If she sent Gunner back to Mike, she could focus on the big stock shows . . . the giants of the Quarter Horse, Paint, and Pinto Worlds. There'd be fewer shows, but each one was a big deal . . . and they led to the one she really wanted – The World Paint Horse Show. She and Mike agreed that Gunner had the quality and the talent to compete at that level, and the schedule worked better for Heather's situation.

2003 was a growing up year for Gunner. From February to July he trained with Mike and Heather and traveled the Gulf Coast in style. The shows they attended – usually one a month – were enormous affairs: the Fort Worth Stock Show and Rodeo in February, the Houston Stock Show and Rodeo in March, off to Louisiana in April, then a warm-up for the Worlds at the Memorial Day Classic in Iowa, the World Pinto Show in Oklahoma in June, and finally, the World Paint Show in Fort Worth in July. Gunner seemed to sense the seriousness of these events, and in the show ring, he put aside his antics and gave his all.

In between events he trained and lived the pampered life of a well-loved show horse. He ate the best feed, enjoyed regular baths and daily grooming, and wore sheets to keep the flies at bay and the sun from bleaching his rich coat. His tail was luxurious and his hooves carefully trimmed and shod. He enjoyed massages and soothing leg wraps, deep bedded stalls, and leisurely playtime in meticulously cared-for paddocks. Gone were the days of muddy pens and rolling pastures full of frisky babies.

This was the big-time!

By the end of that season, Gunner had matured greatly and was looking more promising than ever. He had wracked up several top-ten placings (out of hundreds, in some classes), a reserve championship, and had won a beautiful new saddle. Heather was pleased with him, and with herself for managing to accomplish as much as she had with a busy three year old in tow. Wesley traveled almost everywhere with her and was a going concern in the barns and on the sidelines of the show ring. Always curious, always into something . . . it was like constantly having two Gunners. But Heather loved having Wes there and wouldn't have traded those days with her little son for anything.

After the last show that year, it was time to rest young bones and tired muscles. Gunner enjoyed the autumn with Buttermilk and the other horses, fresh grass, a cozy stable at night, and a bit of freedom to be a regular horse for a while.

That autumn, he got kicked out of the working-horse barn! E.W. kept a string of ranch horses, used at roping events and for work on the farm. They were mostly big, tough, level-headed Quarter horses, used to working hard and staying out of trouble. Gunner was a spirited young show horse with a silky, polished coat and a penchant for trouble. Heather fussed and worried over him and gave E.W. heck every time something happened, as if it were his fault.

One day, Heather brought E.W. a nice lunch and left it in the barn where he would find it when he was finished working. Unfortunately, she had left it sitting a little too close to Gunner's stall, and by the time E.W. came for it, it was completely destroyed. Gunner got caught up in wire that no other horse could have found and gotten into in a million years. He squashed a kitten, broke fence rails, and was constantly wreaking havoc with the other horses.

The trouble was, the problems all seemed to occur when Heather was away working or visiting her mom at the Picayune farm. (Her father had passed away recently and she was spending more time there than usual.) When Heather was home, Gunner was better behaved.

The final straw came one night after Heather returned from a conference to find that the tip of one of Gunner's ears had been bitten off. E.W. heard about that even before Heather had a chance to make it back to the house. Wesley ran ahead of her shouting, "Mama's steaming mad at you, Daddy. Why'd you let Gunner get hurt again?" E.W. was not impressed, and Gunner found himself living in the little show barn in Picayune just a few days later.

The issue remained a running joke between the young couple for the rest of their marriage. E.W. would not allow that sissy show horse in his roping-horse barn, and he was loath to care for him whenever Heather had to be away, knowing that something was bound to happen . . . and something nearly always did!

Not all of Gunner's antics were harmful though. One afternoon, while he was still at the ranch, Heather and E.W. were cleaning stalls in the barn as Wesley played in the stable yard – or so they thought. Gunner and Buttermilk and a few other horses were in the paddock by the barn, where there was a very enticing, large brush pile, just right for exploring.

Suddenly, E.W. and Heather heard a ruckus. They could hear Wesley's squealing and yelling, but couldn't, at first, tell where it was coming from. Then they saw Gunner crashing out from the edge of the brush pile with Wesley dangling – airplane style, arms and legs spread-eagle and "flying" – in front of him. The little horse had Wesley by the back of his pants and Wes was laughing and hollering to beat all.

"Gunner, put him down," shouted Heather, running toward them, and Gunner instantly dropped the boy with a thud. Immediately, the unharmed child was up

and back in the brush pile in hot pursuit of something. Before they could reach him, Gunner had grabbed Wesley again, pulling him down from a high branch and "flying" him back to safety.

Heather was just about to scold the horse *and* the boy, when E.W. noticed a large snake draped across one of the branches, close to where Wes had been exploring. Gunner, it seemed, had not forgotten how to be a hero.

4

All Round Champ

ebruary 2004 found Gunner and Heather heading back to the Will Rogers Equestrian Center in Fort Worth, Texas, for the start of what would be their biggest show year ever. The Fort Worth Stock Show & Rodeo was a massive event, running for over three weeks and providing an important venue for horsemen, cattlemen, rodeo participants, and vendors of ranch and stock breeding related products.

The American Paint Horse is one of the most popular horse breeds in North America due to its steady disposition, attractive, stock-type body, and its beautiful coat patterns. At these big stock shows, the breed is always heavily represented, with hundreds of competitors battling for the top titles and the chance to prove that they have the best of the breed. Now it was Gunner's opportunity to demonstrate just how versatile and superior the breed could be.

There would be no babying him this year. He had grown both mentally and physically and was ready to do the job he had been bred for. Heather began working with him at her mother's farm, and he was fit and sound. Instead of the few classes per show they had entered the previous year, this show season they were chasing the All Round title. That meant Gunner would have to perform in up to twenty classes over the course of a show, in *every* discipline they offered. Points were racked up according to placement in each class, and the horse with the highest score at the end of the show would earn the coveted title.

Heather saw these early season shows as warm-ups, paving the way to the World All Round Paint title, but that didn't mean she wasn't riding to win at each one. She was highly competitive and had the skills to show her horse to his best advantage. She entered the ring every bit as immaculately turned out as her mount, wearing extraordinarily expensive show outfits, and with every hair in place. It was an expensive game she was playing. The travel, the trainer, the top-quality equipment, and the entry fees all added up to thousands, and she was determined to make sure that they earned their right to be there among the elite.

Gunner did not disappoint. He was always playful, always mischievous and full of life in the barns and the practice ring, but when he entered the show ring, he just seemed to know that it was time to be serious. Heather soon came to trust that he would always put in his best effort, and the pair was rewarded for their hard work. Show after show that winter, they received top scores in the classes they entered, and walked away with the all round title. Gunner was on top and getting stronger.

After Fort Worth, Heather went home to Mississippi and Gunner went back into training with Mike Stable. The patient trainer continued to refine the horse's abilities. Side passes and spins, rein backs and higher jumps, head sets and collection . . . there was so much to learn if Gunner were to reach the top. Luckily, Gunner was a fast learner and seemed to enjoy the training and increased demands. If things got too serious, he'd find ways to cut loose and let his trainer know that a little playtime was in order.

By show time, Mike would ship Gunner to the show

site and Heather would meet him there. Heather already knew her horse well and was an exceptionally confident and skilled rider, but she was not so confident as to think she knew it all. Every horse was an individual and every day could bring something unexpected – a mood, a touch of soreness, a sudden burst of energy. When you were dealing with living, breathing, feeling creatures, you took nothing for granted.

So, she would spend hours before the show began, going over her partner, getting to know him again, discovering what he had learned since she'd seen him last, and how she could best support him in his performances. She and Mike could often be found in the practice arena or stable during the wee hours of the morning, perfecting a move, refining a skill or tending to the care of their charge. Nothing was left to chance.

One of Heather's main areas of focus with Gunner was in showmanship. It was the one class in which Heather's performance would be judged rather than Gunner's, and a class where careful training and preparation really paid off.

In showmanship, the exhibitors are scored on their ability to fit and present a horse. Immaculate grooming, instant and lively responses from the horse when asked to walk or trot in hand and "stand square," and top-notch manners from horse and handler alike are essential. A sluggish response, requiring the handler to urge the horse excessively, or excitable behavior, causing the handler to struggle to maintain control, or a sloppy presentation during inspection are fatal mistakes in the showmanship class. In the ring, it looks deceivingly simple, but it requires hours of training and practice, and it was one of Heather's favorites.

This would also be the class that would, eventually, be theirs in a very special way, although, luckily, Heather could not have foreseen the events that would lead to that day.

For now, it was the World Paint Show that was on her mind and with every passing month and every successful show that spring, her hopes grew higher. That ugly, sassy colt was proving to be one of the best!

The World Paint Show in Fort Worth was the one she had set her sights on, but just ahead of it was the World Champion Pinto Show, and it was here that Gunner really came into his own.

Paints and Pintos are often confused, as they share their distinguishing, colorful coat patterns, but they are *not* the same. A Paint is a breed, a specific stock-type horse that can only be registered if both parents are registered with the American Paint Horse Association.

Pinto is a color – a solid colored body with large white splashes in various patterns. Many breeds can have the pinto coloring. There is a registry for Pintos, but it is not a breed in it's own right. Most Paints are Pintos, which is what causes the confusion, but only some Pintos are Paints.

At the World Pinto Show, then, Gunner would be competing against other Paints, but also against many other breeds, some more suited for certain disciplines than the typical stock horse is. These were some of the best of their breeds and competition would be fierce.

When Mike and Heather met up for the show in Tulsa, Oklahoma that June, they were both excited to see what would happen. Gunner had never looked better. After a season of training and showing hard, he was in peak condition and performing with more confidence each time. They both had a feeling that this would be his big year.

Wesley was as much a part of the show scene as the hay and the horses and the trailer they called home for that week. Heather was glad for his company, and pleased to watch her son growing up in the same blessed atmosphere that she had. She was certain that nothing could stop them now. All was well with her world!

Over the course of a week, they worked hard . . .

training into the wee hours of the morning, bathing and grooming Gunner to perfection, cleaning tack to an immaculate shine, preparing Heather's outfits, and taking care of Wesley's needs. Mike had several other horses and clients there that week as well, so he was exceedingly busy the whole time.

Heather had entered Gunner in every class available to them in her age category (19-34 yrs). Gunner held his head low, neck perfectly arched and soft, and walked, jogged and loped through his western pleasure and equitation classes; he picked his way carefully and calmly through the obstacles of the trail class; he came to life in the reining and roping classes, and then showed off his extended trot and jumping style in the hunter and English classes. He was the model of manners in showmanship, and earned top points in the halter class. Eighteen classes and a lot of hard work later, and Heather's ugly duckling was crowned a prince, not only earning the High Point All Round Amateur (19-34 yrs) title but excelling. No other horse even came close to his final score!

For Mike Stable, it was one of the best shows he'd ever had. The horses he'd prepared all did well . . . they cleaned house in almost every All Round category that was available. He couldn't have been more pleased!

They were all tired though. It was nearing the end of the season and they'd been training and showing hard for months now. The week had taken its toll. Even Gunner seemed quieter than usual and wasn't up to his usual pranks. In five days, they'd be back in Fort Worth, Texas to do it all again, but at the moment, everyone needed a rest.

On the final night of the show, after Wesley was tucked into his bunk and asleep in the trailer, Heather went to Gunner's stall to check on him for the night. They'd be on the road again first thing in the morning.

When she entered his stall, he gave her a soft nicker, and she could almost feel his fatigue. The usual toss of his head was missing. The fierce eyes were soft and tired. He didn't come and crowd her and start nipping and nibbling at her, searching for treats, in his usual way. She went to him and rubbed his ears, and he pushed his head into her hands wearily.

She knew that if she asked it of him, Gunner would keep giving his all over the next few weeks. He'd go back to Texas with Mike tomorrow, as planned, and work in the arena every day until they shipped to the Will Rogers Equestrian Center for the World Paint Show. He'd try his best, as he always did, despite his own fatigue, and if he could, he would out-perform them all there too. He would do that because he was Gunner. But Heather also knew that he deserved something better. She pulled out her cell phone and made a quick call, then left Gunner to go find Mike.

Mike was packing equipment into his rig when she found him. He was whistling softly and smiled when she approached. He, too, was tired but elated from the successful week they'd all had.

"I'm taking Gunner with me tomorrow," Heather announced.

Mike straightened from his work, surprised. "You're taking him home? What about the Paint show?"

"No, not home. We're staying here in Oklahoma for a few days. Gunner needs a rest, and I'm taking him to Wes's godfather's place for a little R&R. It'll do him good, and he'll be fresher for the Worlds."

"Okay," Mike agreed reluctantly, "but don't you let anything happen to him. He's as ready as he's ever going to be for that show."

By mid-morning the next day, Gunner was stepping off the trailer and being led to a large, grassy paddock. Like so many show horses, he had barely seen the outside of the barn in months, and for a few moments, he didn't seem to know what to do with his newfound freedom. It didn't take him long to decide, though, and he was soon on his back, rolling and stirring up some dust. When he finally heaved himself back onto his feet, he was covered in soil and his mane was tangled with bits of grass. He shook himself and then went on the search for fresh greens . . . something he'd tasted precious little of in the past few months.

Wes looked at his mother in awe, certain she'd be upset by the grass stains and black smudges on Gunner's gleaming coat. "Mama," he whispered, "Gunner's a mess!"

Heather laughed and looked down at her little boy. "We all need to get messy sometimes, don't we?" she answered. He grinned at her and turned to run and find his godfather.

For the next few days, Gunner got to be a regular horse, sleeping in the sun (without anyone fussing over whether his coat might get sunburned), trotting around his little field, nibbling grass, and rolling in the dirt whenever he chose. After the second day, he was looking for trouble, tossing his head and whinnying whenever Heather came into view, kicking up his heels at every little shadow, and generally, getting back to his old self. Heather was pleased, and she felt much better about taking him to their final show this way, rested and relaxed and ready to put in one last big effort for the season.

They packed up and headed out on the afternoon of

their fourth day there. They had a long haul to go before they hit Texas and the show site, but Heather was feeling rested too, and ready.

It was late when they hit the state line and Heather called Mike. She didn't want anyone but Mike to see Gunner when she brought him to the barn that night . . . and she knew that even quiet, gentle Mike was going to have a fit.

"We should be there around 2 a.m.," she told him.

"Great! I didn't want to sleep tonight anyway," Mike answered sarcastically.

"Aw, you'd have been up anyway. This will just give you something to do," Heather teased. "See you in a couple of hours."

The stable was quiet when they arrived. Mike was waiting, and when Heather unloaded Gunner, Mike groaned loudly. "Heather, what on earth happened to him?" he asked, shocked by the muddy, unkempt bush pony in front of him.

Heather grinned sheepishly. "He got to be a horse for a few days," she answered. "And now we get to turn him back into a champ before morning!"

And so began the 2004 World Paint Show – starting with a trip to the wash rack at three o'clock in the morning.

A few days rest had made the world of difference, and Gunner seemed livelier than ever. Almost too lively. In the wash rack, he grabbed at the hose as they soaked and scrubbed and rinsed him, sending water spraying everywhere and ensuring that they were all soaked before that bath was done. He refused to stand still as they tried to straighten his mane and nipped as they polished his hooves. Heather and Mike were cursing him before they finally had him back in show condition, but they were also pleased. If Gunner was being bad, it meant he was feeling good. And he was definitely feeling good now!

He continued to pull pranks throughout the week, nearly driving them insane with his antics. In the practice ring, just before a hunter class they were entered in, Heather turned him toward a low jump that he had seen a dozen times before and asked him to take it. Just as they approached the jump, he came to a sliding halt, sending her flying over his head and pile-driving her into the rails. Mike was there at once, checking to see if she was all right. Luckily, nothing was hurt except her pride, and when Heather turned to her mount, it was just as it had been so long ago in the ranch yard when they had first met. His head was turned so that he faced her with his one blue eye, challenging but cautious, and

she stared back at him, her own dark eyes flashing with anger. They squared off that way for several long minutes before Gunner lowered his head and came forward a step, lips twitching and ears relaxed to the sides in surrender.

Mike helped brush Heather off and remount, then he led them to the ring, where the class was about to enter. As always, Gunner put aside all play when he stepped inside, and they came out of the class with top scores.

At the end of the week, they were once again awarded the All Round title in their category, the prize that Heather had been longing for so much. Now they could head home for a well-deserved break.

Gunner enjoyed the remainder of that summer and autumn in more relaxed fashion, although, with another show season coming up in just six months, he was not left to become grass-fat and sunburned. Heather continued to work with him several times a week, as much to keep him sharp and fit as to teach him new skills now. Occasionally, she and E.W. would take him to a small, local show, or a roping show and try him out there (and endure the constant teasing about having her baby in with the "real" horses), or ride him for pleasure, but mostly, he was a show horse and enjoyed a pampered life.

Wesley started school that autumn and spent most afternoons at his grandmother Maria's house in Picayune, waiting for his mom to pick him up on her way home from her nursing job in New Orleans before they made the drive to their ranch in Laurel. During those weeks with his grandma, Wes became one of Gunner's favorite people. The boy shared donuts with him and Buttermilk, played with them over the fence, and just seemed to always be around, chattering and providing a little excitement and stimulation in their otherwise quiet days.

At Wes's side, at almost all times, was a little Schnauzer called Tramp, who Wes and E.W. had brought home from a roping show that summer. Heather had been furious at yet another stray being brought home and had, at first, insisted that they get rid of him. But the dog was still there a few days later, and as she watched her son play and fall in love with the little creature, she resigned herself to the fact that it was staying. The dog had worked its way into their lives and into Heather's heart, and now it was with them wherever they went. Like Gunner, this was not a working ranch dog, kennelled and tough and scrappy. This was a family member and enjoyed a much more pampered existence.

To look out the window of Maria's house and see the dog Tramp, Wes, and Gunner playing together that autumn was a perfectly normal, everyday sight, but one that stirred the heart every time.

Gunner would wait each day for Wes to arrive, eager for the donuts and other treats the boy always had. He would nicker as soon as he saw him and become rowdy if Wes didn't come to him right away. Likewise, if Heather was away for more than a day, Gunner would start getting into trouble, as though complaining about her lack of attention. When she returned to the farm after a few days' absence, it was often to listen to the irritated rantings of her mother, complaining about "that horse."

"He reached over the fence and ate the passenger side mirror right off my truck!" "He's squashed another chicken! At this rate, I'll have no hens left before he heads back to Texas." One of Gunner's favorite things to do was to squash chickens to death. If one wandered into his stall or paddock, he would line it up, lower his great mass, and roll on it. Then he'd just lay there, maybe until he could no longer feel it struggling, before he'd get back to his feet and go about his business, leaving behind the smothered, flattened carcass of the poor hen (and once a cat).

He still enjoyed the occasional escape, and if he was feeling particularly sassy, he could still nip or annoy his human friends in a hundred little ways. This was always worse when he was missing Heather and Wes. When they were around, he never seemed quite so bad.

They did make it through that winter, squashed chickens and all, and soon they were preparing for another show season to begin. Heather was working harder with him now, getting him ready for the first big stock show in Texas, where they would meet Mike Stable and start another round. Heather was sure that 2005 would be as good as, or better than, the previous year. Gunner was at his best – rested, spirited, and eager to work again. He was responsive under saddle, and talented in so many ways. Heather intended to continue their winning streak of 2004.

Heather's first concern was always for the health and welfare of her horse, but she pushed hard, prepared thoroughly, and poured whatever money she needed to into the game. She had high expectations, all of which paid off as they made their way through that show season, cleaning up again and again. Heather, with Wesley and Tramp and Mike by her side at all times, was proud of her horse and delighted to have a partner who could take her this far and be this much fun. At times, it seemed as though nothing on earth could get in their way. They were on the top and flying.

They completed that show season as a force to be reckoned with and already looked forward to the next season. Gunner had worked very hard all spring and summer, had dominated the competition in all of the shows they entered, and headed home in August, ready for some peace and quiet. Little did they know that he was soon to face the biggest challenge he'd ever come up against. Within weeks of coming home, he was in a competition for his life.

5

The Week of Katrina

ugust 23, 2005 – Heather and Gunner were attending a small show in Louisiana when Heather heard on the news that Tropical Depression 12 had formed over the Bahamas. She had registered the information, but paid little attention. Tropical depressions sometimes form into tropical storms or even hurricanes, but at that point, Heather had classes to get through and hot, humid weather to contend with.

August 24 – The tropical depression began to gain

strength and was upgraded to a tropical storm and named Katrina.

Heather and Gunner completed the show in top form by the end of this day and were preparing for the trip home. Heather kept an ear on the news, but still not too anxiously. Hurricanes are part of the landscape in Louisiana. They are taken seriously, but people don't tend to panic over them. Until danger is imminent, it's business as usual.

Tropical Storm Katrina moved steadily toward Florida throughout the day, picking up strength as it went. It was upgraded to a Category 2 hurricane just hours before it hit Florida.

August 25 – Katrina weakened back to a tropical storm as it traveled over land, but regained hurricane status within an hour of entering the warm waters of the Gulf of Mexico. This was the third major hurricane in the region that season, but this one would be different.

Heather and Gunner headed for home.

August 26 – Meteorologists predicted that Katrina would head toward the Florida Panhandle, but unusually warm waters and a strong weather system was making the storm's path difficult to predict. Gulf Coast residents became uneasy when Katrina did not turn, as predicted, and started heading their way, gaining power as she came.

At the ranch in Laurel, and on the farm in Picayune, the first preparations were beginning to be made . . . just in case. Both locations were inland enough to be relatively safe, but people had been through enough hurricanes to know how much damage the high winds and heavy rains could cause, even far in from the coast.

August 27 – Katrina intensified to a Category 3 hurricane and was now bearing down on the Gulf Coast states. A hurricane watch was started for South East Louisiana, including New Orleans and the Mississippi and Alabama coasts. The storm was temporarily slowed by a disturbance, but the disturbance doubled the size of the system, making Katrina a very different kind of hurricane – the "big one." The watch was upgraded to a warning, and as the storm, now twice as large, began to regain power and move toward the Louisiana coast, people became very nervous. The president declared a federal state of emergency in the region and prepared to send in troops to assist if the devastation was as great as forecasters were starting to fear.

Heather and E.W. decided that Gunner would be

safer at the Laurel ranch than in the stable at Picayune. Laurel is farther inland, and horses, given enough space and natural cover, can usually make it through severe weather better outside than indoors. In a hurricane, they have been known to huddle or even lie down as a group to withstand the winds. Gunner, Buttermilk, and the other horses from Maria's stable were trailered to the ranch that afternoon and turned out in a large pasture with a wide creek in the middle and plenty of sheltered areas.

Heather had to report to the hospital in New Orleans. Touro Hospital was under high alert and every available body was needed to prepare for the onslaught of victims they knew would come with a storm as massive and powerful as this one.

At the ranch, E.W. and Wes worked hard to tie down, secure, cover, and otherwise protect everything they could.

August 28 – Katrina was upgraded to a Category 4 hurricane at two in the morning. Five hours later, it was a Category 5 hurricane and was packing sustained winds of incredible strength. The storm was a monster now, and by 9:30 a.m. the government, now facing one of the largest and most powerful hurricanes to ever hit the

Gulf Coast, decided to issue the first-ever mandatory evacuation orders for large areas of South East Louisiana and coastal Mississippi and Alabama. Forty-one counties and sixty-one cities were ordered to evacuate, including the city of New Orleans, which was in grave peril. No one knew if the city's levees would hold under the rapidly approaching conditions . . . and if they didn't, the entire city could soon be under water.

Over a million people began moving inland, with only hours between them and the fierce storm. At 4:30 p.m., the National Weather Service issued a special hurricane warning: *In the likely event of a Category 4 or 5 hit, most of the area will be uninhabitable for weeks, perhaps longer. . . . At least one-half of well-constructed homes will have roof and wall failure. All gabled roofs will fail, leaving those homes severely damaged or destroyed. . . . Power outages will last for weeks. . . . Water shortages will make human suffering incredible by modern standards.*

August 29 – Katrina made landfall near Buras, Louisiana, at 6:10 a.m. with high winds and extremely heavy rains. Her swath of winds, from the eye of the storm outward, was more than a hundred miles wide, and her winds were beyond ferocious. She destroyed everything in her path.

Katrina weakened slightly to a Category 3 as she moved overland and into Breton Sound, before making her third landfall near the Louisiana/Mississippi border. Storm swells battered the coast, and at 7:30 a.m., New Orleans' levees were reported as being breached. Soon water began to flood over 80 percent of the city.

The storm raged on, maintaining Category 3 hurricane strength until she was well into Mississippi. The eye of the storm passed over Picayune and Laurel, with winds still raging at a hundred and twenty miles per hour. Every county in Mississippi suffered destruction.

At Touro Hospital, Heather was so busy that she barely had time to think about what might be happening at home, which was a blessing because she was worried sick. She had phoned home as often as she could when the storm hit, but now the phone lines were down, and she had no way of knowing what was happening. Earlier, she had spoken to E.W. and he told her that he and Wes were camping in the hallway, as it seemed like the safest place in the house. Shortly after, when she called again, E.W. informed her that a tree had crashed through their roof, and he was taking Wes to the big hay barn.

"Don't worry," he soothed. "I'll take good care of him. We'll be waiting for you. We'll be all right." Then the lines went dead. She'd been unable to get through since.

Around the same time, Maria had phoned them to see how they were making out. Wes came on the line. "Hi Grandma. Mama's going to be upset. Our living room curtains are all gone." Before she could find out exactly what that meant, they were cut off. She had her own storm to survive, as the little farm was being battered, but she was very worried, both for her son-in-law and grandson in Laurel, and for her daughter in New Orleans, where reports of levee breaches, severe flooding, and desperate conditions were already beginning to emerge. She prayed that they would all find each other safe and sound in the days ahead.

6

Lost in the Storm

The following days were ones of chaos. The entire Gulf Coast had been affected, much of it damaged beyond recognition. People lost homes, family members, pets, and all of their belongings. Relief shelters were filled to capacity and in need of help. Every hospital in New Orleans had been forced to close, except Touro, where exhausted staff were working long hours with no electricity, no running water, and no relief from the hot and humid weather that followed Katrina. The damage to that beautiful city was extensive and the focus in the days following the monster storm was on rescuing and treating those who had been left behind during the evacuation.

In the week following Katrina's landfall, Heather worked doggedly alongside the other health-care workers who remained in New Orleans. Communications were completely down, and roads and transportation systems were non-functional, so she had no way of finding out if her family was all right. Horror stories of lost loved ones were flooding the corridors of the hospital, and Heather could only hope they had made it through safely.

In Picayune, Maria's farm was safe. The house had made it through unscathed. The barn roof was ruined but repairable. But she, too, was isolated, with no means of reaching her daughter, the ranch, or other family members. She was desperately worried.

When E.W. and Wes emerged after the storm finally died down, their world had completely changed. A large tree had smashed through the middle of their house and almost every window had been blown out. The heavy rains had poured in and many belongings were ruined.

The big hay barn, where they had been sheltered, sustained little damage, while another, beside it, was torn to pieces. Trees were down, farm items were scattered – sometimes surprising distances from where they had started – and everything was under water. Long stretches of fencing were destroyed. It was almost too much to take in. E.W. barely knew where to start.

It took an enormous effort to get his emotions in check and smile down at little Wes, who was staring around with wide eyes.

"Looks like we have a lot of work to do before Mama comes home," E.W. said, as cheerily as he could. He was hoping beyond hope that Heather *would* be coming home. He had no way of knowing how she was, and he was extremely worried.

Luckily, the horse trailer made a very comfortable temporary home. It was a luxury model with a complete apartment in the front end, and Wes had lived in it often enough while on the road with his mother. E.W. made it into an adventure, and the pair of them gathered food and clothes and water from their damaged house and set up their new home for a long-term stay.

Over the next few days, they took stock of the situation on the rest of the farm. They were constantly amazed by how far the hurricane had blown so many heavy items. The long, slow process of cleaning up began. They cared for the animals that had survived the storm, and buried the ones that did not. They repaired fences to hold the ones that staggered back home and began to ride out each day in search of the ones that were still lost. Many cattle were missing, and some of the horses had crossed downed fence lines and were found in the far reaches of the ranch or on neighboring farms. Some were injured and needed attention. Within a week, they had found almost all of the lost animals, but one horse was still missing. Even after days of searching, E.W. could not find Gunner anywhere.

The other horses in Gunner's pasture were still there. All E.W. could figure was that before the storm, Gunner must have crossed the broad stream that ran through the middle of the field, probably on one of his curious adventures. When Katrina's rains had come and turned the stream into a wide and fast-running river, he could not get back and had wandered off in an attempt to escape the frightening winds and flying debris. He was a pampered show horse, after all. He was like a captive animal, suddenly set free to fend for himself. His chances of survival when on the loose were far below those of a naturally kept horse.

In New Orleans, Heather was oblivious to all of this, but growing more desperate for word about her husband, son, and mother with every passing day. She and the other care providers at the hospital were working in grim conditions. Touro was still the only hospital open in the whole of New Orleans, and their resources were quickly running low. They were evacuating as many of the movable patients as they could, but the beds were full and hurricane victims would continue to arrive for weeks to come. Temperatures were sweltering – almost unbearable – and there was no air conditioning or running water. Electricity production from the generators was testy and fragile. Medical supplies and fresh water were running low. Heather caught sleep when she could and tried to maintain sanity when she was awake. All she really wanted was to go home and see her family.

After a full, agonizing week, Heather had the opportunity to have contact with home. Sanderson Farms, one of the largest and richest chicken producers in the United States, was based out of Laurel and employed E.W. The enormous farm had suffered its own severe losses, with millions of chickens killed in the hurricane, but they possessed a means of transport that would become vital to the relief effort in New Orleans. They became a major contributor in many ways over the coming months.

The medical team stranded in Touro hospital could not just drive away to check on their homes and families. Most of their vehicles were under water, the roads were flooded or badly damaged, and hospital workers were expected to remain within contact range until the worst of the emergency was under control. That could be weeks! But the Sanderson's Blackhawk jet helicopters could get people to and from the hospital for short periods, and in this way, Heather was finally brought home.

Heather was shocked to find her house destroyed and appalled by the amount of damage to the farm and surrounding area. She learned that the eye of the storm had passed directly over Laurel, and while they were far enough away from the coast to be protected from the storm surge that had devastated New Orleans and other coastal communities, the fierce winds and rain had taken a huge toll. There was no community in Mississippi that was unaffected.

Despite all of this, she was overjoyed . . . so grateful to hold her son and husband in her arms again. She tried, unsuccessfully, to reach her mother in Picayune, but communications had not yet been restored. It would be *another* week before she would hear her voice and know she was fine.

Heather could only stay for a short visit before heading back to the hospital, but it was long enough to rejuvenate her for the grueling weeks ahead. E.W. didn't mention Gunner's disappearance. All Heather was concerned about at that point was keeping her family safe. She had never contemplated losing them before, and to come so close changed the way she looked at everything. Her gratitude was immense. To face that kind of natural power and be blessed enough to see the following day with your family safe and unharmed seemed like nothing short of a miracle.

Heather, E.W., and Wes would call the horse trailer home for the next six weeks, which meant they were better off than many in the region. At least their home was repairable. At least they had each other and a way to stay on their own land in the meantime. So many people lost everything, including loved ones, and the Goodwin family was grateful for all they had.

They would remain cut off from the rest of the world, without running water or electricity for another three weeks. Their fuel supply was limited, and the roads were so damaged and blocked with fallen trees, downed power lines, and other debris that travel was next to impossible. The Sanderson helicopter was Heather's only means of transport back and forth, and she was only able to stay for a day or two at the most, but every time she returned, she could see how hard E.W. and Wes had been working to get their lives back in order.

E.W. continued to ride out almost daily in search of missing animals, including Gunner, but there was no trace of the colorful gelding. When he finally told Heather, she was devastated. Her focus had been entirely on her family and her patients, but now it felt as though a child were missing from their family. When she was able, she joined in the search for him, and prayed that somehow, he would have survived.

Although ranch life slowly began to take some form again over the next month, the situation remained desperate in New Orleans – and would for a long time to come. Heather was constantly exhausted, moving between the shattered city and her life in a horse trailer. Sometimes she would go only as far as Picayune and rest there, where Wes was staying with his Grandma Maria much of the time now.

Try as she did to maintain hope, as the months went by with no sign of her horse, Heather began to doubt that they would ever see Gunner alive again. There was no saying what kind of trouble he may have gotten himself into. As Christmas approached, they all began to admit that the chances of his return were less than slim.

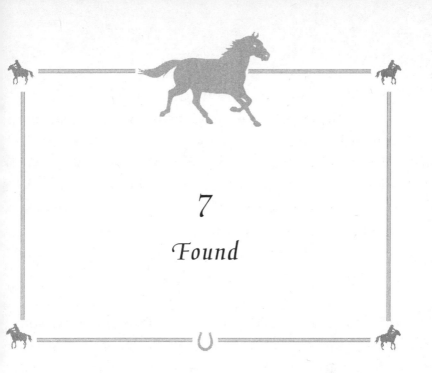

7

Found

Heather was surprised beyond belief on December 26, when E.W. phoned her at the hospital to say he'd just received a phone call from an animal rescue group in Waynesboro, two counties and over thirty miles east of them. A horse had staggered into an elderly lady's yard in the town, and when she had tried to chase it out of her garden with a broom, it had collapsed and couldn't get back up. She had phoned the sheriff, and the horse had been transported to the rescue station. The veterinarian there had examined him and found a microchip implant that had helped them identify him. It was Gunner.

Unfortunately, they were calling with the recommendation to put him out of his misery. He was malnourished, dehydrated, extremely weak, and badly injured. The vet felt that the extent of his suffering made his chances of a successful recovery very poor. They were waiting now for the go-ahead from Heather.

For Heather, though, this was out of the question.

"Tell them not to do anything. I'm coming," she told E.W.

E.W. tried to talk her out of it. "Heather, it'll take you hours, and he's suffering. They said he's in really bad shape. The roads are still a mess east of here. . . . You'll have to go around by the back roads to get there. Why don't you just let them deal with it?"

"No. He's hung on for three months. Who am I to give up on him! Tell them I'm on my way."

The following hours were extremely chaotic. By then, Heather had a vehicle again, but the roads in and out of New Orleans were still nearly impassable. The drive to Picayune, which under normal conditions took about forty minutes, now took her close to three hours. Wes was there, and while Heather hitched the trailer, he insisted on going with her. At first she resisted. She wasn't sure exactly how they were going to get there, or just how bad Gunner would be. But Wes was very much his mother's son and would not take no for an answer.

"All right," she finally relented, "but be prepared for a long, hard night!"

To her mother, Maria, she instructed, "Call Dr. White and tell her we're going to need her. I'll phone you when we're getting close. And get a stall ready. I'm bringing him home if I can."

Maria also tried to talk her out of the rescue mission, but Heather would have none of it. "I have to see him for myself. I *will not* give up on him until I know for sure."

It took them over five hours to travel the thirty miles to Waynesboro. They were forced to detour around broken bridges, washed out roads, and storm-ravaged terrain. It had been more than eight hours since they had received the call. Heather hoped they had been able to make Gunner somewhat comfortable and that he was still hanging on.

Tears filled her eyes when she finally saw him. He was emaciated, so weak he could barely stand, and one eye was swollen and infected. He was scraped and bruised and very dirty, but it was definitely Gunner. He raised his head ever so slightly at the sound of her voice. That was enough to make her want to try.

"I'm taking him home," she announced.

Getting him home would be a lot easier said than done, however. Gunner was too weak to walk onto the trailer on his own, and they ended up having to use a hoist to get him into a cattle trailer, instead. This whole process took all the energy he had left, and he could not stand for the journey home.

The drive back to Picayune was agonizingly slow and nerve-wracking. Heather was tense and whispered, "I'm sorry," at every bump and bend in the damaged road, knowing that Gunner was feeling every jolt. "Just make it home, Gunner. Then it'll be all right," she encouraged him over and over, although he could not hear her.

When they finally pulled into the yard at Picayune, the vet, Dr. Anne White, and Maria were there, waiting. Gunner had managed to get to his feet when the trailer stopped, and now staggered onto solid ground very unsteadily.

"Oh my," breathed Dr. White, approaching to put a steadying hand on his side. She gave Heather a look that told her to prepare for the worst.

Two things helped Heather make up her mind in the next few minutes. First, her mom smiled at her and said "He doesn't look quite as bad as I expected." Heather could have laughed – or cried – she wasn't sure which would come more easily. She had watched her mother mend injured dogs, children, broken hearts, and many, many horses over the years. If anyone could pull Gunner through, it was Maria.

The other deciding factor came from Gunner himself. Wes stood by the trailer with tears streaming down his face while Gunner was being unloaded.

"Is Gunner gonna die?" he sobbed.

At the sound of the boy's voice, Gunner stopped and nickered, soft and low, as though to comfort him. That clinched it. They had to try.

"No honey," Heather said, smiling encouragingly at her young son. Poor Wes had been through so much lately. "Gunner's going to be okay. He'll be sick for a while though, and we have to take good care of him."

Gunner would be sick for a long while! The effort of getting into the barn was too much, and as he turned in his stall, he went down again. They knew that without intensive help, he would soon be unable to rise at all. He had very little left.

The emergency room nurse in Heather kicked in as she assisted Dr. White in starting an intravenous line and hooking up a bag of nutrient-rich fluids to start rehydrating Gunner's depleted body.

They set up a body sling, supported by the barn rafters, and a pulley system to help Gunner stand. Horses

spend the vast majority of time on their feet, even sleeping standing up. They cannot be off their feet for extended periods of time without suffering life-threatening damage to their hooves. A special structure in their hooves, a triangular, spongy bulb called the frog, works like a pump to force blood through the hoof and lower leg. Blood is pumped with every step the horse takes, and without this vital blood flow, a hoof suffers very serious damage.

They wrapped Gunner's lower legs with support bandages to try to prevent fluid from building up and to assist with standing.

With Gunner now supported by the sling and the IV in place, Dr. White was able to conduct a more detailed examination.

Gunner's right eye was badly damaged and now infected. He had likely been struck by blowing debris during the hurricane and had been coping with the painful, untreated injury for all those weeks. The extent of his suffering must have been terrible. Partially blinded, he would have tried to seek shelter, food, and water, only to find a confusing and unfamiliar land-scape. How he had gone unnoticed all this time, and how he had made his way to Waynesboro was anybody's guess. Along the way he had gathered many scrapes, gouges, and one deep laceration on a hind leg, but he had survived – barely. The following hours and days would be critical.

Dr. White added strong doses of antibiotics and painkillers to the IV "soup" already coursing through Gunner, and then left Heather and Maria with instructions for his care. They blanketed him to reduce the effects of shock. They offered him small amounts of hay and water, but he was too weak to do more than nibble just a little of it. There was a long road ahead for the pretty Paint . . . but first, he had to make it through the night.

8

The Long Road Forward

Gunner did survive that night, and the IV fluids made a world of difference to their patient. Although he was nowhere near strong enough to go without the sling yet, he seemed brighter, his eyes were less sunken, and Heather felt certain that she had made the right choice. What they needed now was time to get nutrients into him and to help him regain his strength. They'd also need a lot of luck so they wouldn't run into secondary problems with internal organs or with his feet.

Over the coming days, Gunner slowly began to come

back. Heather was still working very hard at the hospital and had to be up by 3:30 a.m. to change Gunner's IV bag, get herself ready, and leave the house by 4:30 a.m. if she was going to be at work by 7:30 a.m.

Maria was working to get her school up and running again, but most of Gunner's care fell to her throughout the day. He was beginning to eat a little more hay each day and was gradually able to spend more and more time out of the body sling, although they continued to support him in it for a couple of weeks. Maria groomed him and bathed his damaged eye and dressed his wounds, and gave him what he needed the most . . . a soothing voice and a gentle hand. Outwardly, he was beginning to heal, but he was very quiet. The spirited young horse was no longer there. His ordeal had taken such a lot out of him.

As exhausted as she was, Heather would arrive home late and spend time with Wes and Gunner and her mother. She was devoted to Gunner's care and pitched in as best she could. On the days when she didn't work, she took over his care entirely.

Weeks passed, and Gunner began to put on weight and no longer needed the sling. He was able to get out now for short walks and a bit of paddock time with his buddy, Buttermilk. He was still eating only hay and a bit of fresh grass. Heather and Dr. White agreed that starting him on grain too soon could lead to laminitis, an inflammation of the hooves, especially if the circulation had been compromised for any length of time before they'd gotten him on his feet. Every gain had to be approached gradually, and Heather waited until the end of January before she began offering him small bran mashes. Gunner had always dug into his grain greedily, but now he picked and nibbled and ate halfheartedly.

His lack of spirit became a larger issue for Heather than his physical wounds. His eye had cleared with the antibiotic treatments and care, but it was dull now – black and visionless. It didn't seem to be paining him any longer. But the good eye, that fierce blue eye that had challenged her so boldly at times, was also dull. He did what he was directed to do. He ate what he was given to eat. But there was very little life behind his actions. Heather greatly missed her sassy, bossy colt.

At times, there would be subtle reminders that he was still there inside. Sometimes, he rested his head against them as they changed a leg wrap or nickered a soft greeting when they came into the barn. He leaned into the brush as they cleaned and cared for him. He watched as they worked around the barn. It wasn't much yet, but it was something. Heather hoped that, with time, they'd start to see more and more of him.

By mid-February, almost six months after the hurricane, Heather began to notice her mother complaining about "that horse." "That horse will not keep his leg wraps on," she'd say. "I straighten them out in the morning, and by lunch he's got them all pulled off, trampled in the shavings, and tangled around his legs."

One day she came home to find her mother grinning, but trying to act annoyed. "That horse squashed another one of my hens!" she announced, and Heather burst out laughing. Gunner was back.

With every passing day now, Gunner was gaining strength and his old personality was shining through. The only difference was that he was more affectionate than ever before, demanding attention and raising a ruckus if he didn't get it. He was digging into his feed with vigor again and beginning to play with the other horses when he was turned out. He was skittish on his blind side now, and they had to be more careful about how they approached and handled him, but he seemed to be adjusting and finding his way back.

Competing wasn't even a thought for Heather that year, with Gunner or any other horse. Between rebuilding their lives in Laurel, working in what remained of New Orleans, and caring for Gunner and Wes, there

seemed little room for anything like play. Heather was much like Gunner. She had survived the ordeal and was healing, but she was looking at life through a new set of eyes. It would take a while before she found where she fit again.

It was hard seeing the reality every day – the thousands of people who had lost family, homes, pets, and all they had cherished. So many of them didn't have the resources to rebuild their shattered lives as she had been so lucky to be able to do. She was enormously grateful for the blessing of still having all of her family and even her horse returned to her, but she was changed, like everyone and everything around her.

If some things had been torn apart by Katrina, friendships had been forged and strengthened. The people who had worked alongside Heather at Touro Hospital for all those desperate months had become as close as family to her. They knew each other's stories and had shared many tears, hugs, laughs, and life-changing moments together. One of these friends, Brent Becknow, had heard Gunner's story and was keen to meet this miracle horse. One day, in June 2006, he finally did, and it would mark a new beginning for Heather and Gunner.

It was a pleasantly warm afternoon, and Gunner was out

in his field with Buttermilk, grazing contentedly like a horse that's never known a care in the world. Brent was not a horseman and admitted that he would not have been able to pick Gunner out from any of the other horses. He could see nothing wrong with him from where he stood. He was certainly striking . . . his gleaming golden coat with its odd splashes of white caught the eye, but beyond that, he saw nothing unusual. At least, not until Heather called to him.

At the sound of her voice, his blazed head shot up and turned so that one fierce blue eye faced them. The look was intense and, for a second, Brent felt goose bumps rise on his arms. Gunner arched his neck and, tossing his pretty head, nickered deeply, breaking into a trot to meet them at the fence.

As Brent watched the greeting between Heather and her horse, he saw, for the first time in his life, what a horse/human partnership – one might even say *friendship* – looked like. Without words, the pair was communicating clearly, and the affection between them was unmistakable. It wasn't merely human affection for an animal that was owned, but a genuine affection for a partner and friend, and Gunner returned it in kind.

To Brent's further amazement, Heather and Gunner began what looked to him like some sort of a dance. She moved a hand; he took a step back. She stepped to one side; he stepped the other way. She turned and jogged down the fence line; he immediately broke into a brisk trot and followed at her side. She turned; he turned. She faced him and he stopped, alert to her every move. She pointed a toe, and he shifted a hoof. Brent was spellbound.

"What was that?" he asked when Heather was once again beside him.

She laughed self-consciously and answered, "Oh, it's just a bit of showmanship stuff. We mess around with it all the time. He seems to like it. He's always liked to play games like that."

"You mean that's the sort of thing you'd do at a show?" Brent pressed.

"Yes, sort of . . . in the showmanship class at least. It's all about anticipating each other's cues and moves. It's fun. It's too bad that his show days are over. He was really good."

Brent looked puzzled and asked, "Why are they over? He's looking great from what I can see. Why don't you take him back?"

Heather frowned. "Not with that eye," she answered. "Things are different now. Besides, chasing titles? What does that even mean anymore? It's hard to remember why it was so important, somehow."

Brent thoughtfully watched Gunner, walking quietly back to Buttermilk. Things might have changed for everyone, but he believed in jumping right back into life if things were ever to be normal again. He knew Heather had been through a lot in these past months. They all had. But here was her chance to start again. He said no more then, but a plan was forming in his mind.

Two weeks later, Heather was herded into the staff room at the hospital. She found herself surrounded by a group of grinning friends. Brent's smile was the widest of them all.

"What?" she asked suspiciously.

One of the ladies handed her a card. "An early birthday present," she announced.

Heather looked from the eager faces around her to the card in her hands. Half expecting something to explode or pop out of it, she opened the envelope slowly. Inside the card were papers with the World Paint Show emblem on the letterhead. She glanced over the contents, and then looked up, puzzled.

"I don't get it," she said, looking straight at Brent. "I told you I'm not going to the Worlds this year. Why did you buy my entrance fee? I don't have a horse to enter."

"Yes, you do," said Brent confidently. "You have

Gunner! We entered you and Gunner!"

Heather was dumbfounded and, at first, could hardly comprehend what her friend was suggesting. She decided to phone Mike Stable and see what he thought.

"Great! I'll meet up with you there. I'm taking a few in," said Mike.

"But Gunner's still underweight and he's not fit and . . . his eye! He hasn't had a saddle on him in almost a year," Heather argued.

"Well, get a saddle on him. Just come and have fun. It'll do you both good."

9

A True Champion

With only a week to prepare, Heather and Gunner got ready to go back to the Worlds. It would be Heather's tenth World Paint Show, but she had never done it quite like this. Usually it was months of training, thousands of dollars, high-level competition, and intensely serious. Now they were going just to play, just because they loved to be there, and it felt like the craziest thing she had ever done. By the time they were ready to go, Heather was excited. It was like being a kid on her favorite pony in a 4-H show again.

Wes and his little dog, Tramp, would travel to the Worlds with Heather again that year . . . and so would Brent Becknow. Heather insisted that he come and be her stable-hand, since it had been his crazy idea to go in the first place. He had readily agreed, thinking he was in for a bit of an easy adventure, but it would turn out to be a real education.

It was Brent's first time at *any* horse show, and the sheer size and magnitude of this one was stunning. He dressed up on their first day, expecting to sit up in the stands and watch as Heather and Gunner and all the other magnificent competitors "did their thing," but Heather soon set him straight.

"You're no good to me hanging around the stands," she complained. "Go put on some work clothes and meet me in the barn."

What Brent soon learned was that these big shows were all about the horse. Even though Heather had come in a less competitive frame of mind this year, she still planned to give the few classes they had entered her best shot, and Gunner's care and comfort was her number one concern.

The days started early – far earlier then Brent was prepared for! Bleary eyed, Heather had him cleaning stalls, lugging water buckets, hay bales and bedding, and mixing complicated grain rations. He helped her bathe and groom their charge, polishing hooves, removing grass and urine and mud stains from the white patches on Gunner's coat, and taming a mane and tail that had been allowed to grow wild over the past months. Going from pasture-pretty to show-gorgeous was a lot more work then Brent could ever have guessed. Tack needed to be cleaned, Gunner needed time out of his stall to exercise, and the whole process seemed to be repeated several times a day.

Mike Stable greeted Heather warmly when he saw her, and seemed delighted to find Gunner back in good form.

"Well, he's not what he was before," Heather cautioned. "He's really skittish on his blind side now. That may be a problem when the judges come up on that side in the showmanship class. And he's not in very good shape. But he's alive, and he's here. That's a lot more than I could have hoped for not too long ago."

Mike assured her that they would do fine, and then asked if she was ready. He was used to her being extremely organized, polished, and driven, so he was surprised when she laughed and answered, "No, not quite. I don't have an outfit yet."

He frowned and pulled the class schedule out of his

pocket. "What are you in? Showmanship and hunter, right? They're both tomorrow afternoon!"

"Yup," she answered with a grin. "I'll pick up some stuff when the vendors open in the morning."

Mike laughed. "Oh boy, when I said just come and play, I didn't think you'd take me this literally. It's sure good to see you both back here though."

"It feels great to be here," she admitted.

The next day felt like one disaster after another to Brent, but again, he was learning. This was show life, and southern horse people were a resilient bunch. If they could survive Category 5 hurricanes, they could laugh off the minor catastrophes of a typical, high-stress show day with ease.

Heather had them up at the break of dawn, preparing for the day ahead. Gunner needed to be groomed to perfection and his stall kept spotless to prevent stains on his coat.

Gunner seemed to sense the excitement and was trying them with his old-time pranks. He fooled around in the wash rack and managed to soak both Brent and Heather. He untied himself while they were working on his legs and began wandering down the aisle, visiting other horses and raising a ruckus before they could catch him and get him back to his tie ring. He tipped a water bucket, nipped Tramp, and was just being a general nuisance. Heather couldn't have been more pleased!

She left Brent in charge of him for a while so that she could run to the vendors and buy a show outfit to wear. Brent was in a sweat the whole time, worrying that something would go wrong. Everything was fine, but by the time they began to prepare for the afternoon classes, Brent was exhausted – and the fun had only just begun.

About an hour before their hunter class, Heather took Gunner out to the practice ring to lunge him and warm up his muscles and burn off a bit of his high spirits. He was frisky and playful and, while goofing around, he took a misstep and fell hard. Instead of springing to his feet as he normally would, he stayed down, and for a moment, Heather panicked, thinking he was seriously hurt. Brent was at her side in a moment, eager to do what he could to help.

A minute later, though, Gunner heaved himself to his feet and stood quietly . . . perhaps a little sheepishly . . . as Heather inspected him from top to toe for scrapes and bruises. She had Brent walk and trot him out so she could check for any sign of lameness. He seemed fine. "I think he just knocked the wind out himself," she said, relieved. They headed back to the barn to prepare for the hunter class.

Once again they groomed him, removing every trace of dust from his coat, and saddled him and tied him in his stall to wait a few more minutes before they would head out to the warm-up ring. But the mischievous gelding didn't feel like standing around. He got down in his stall and rolled, saddle and all. Heather let out a yell when she saw what he was doing and urged him back to his feet. He stood before them, his mane sticking up wildly, his tail and saddle pad full of wood shavings. Heather could only laugh . . . this was so Gunner! But Brent was horrified. With only fifteen minutes before their class was due to be called, they worked to clean him up *again* and get him out to the ring for at least a short warm-up.

Despite all of this, Gunner held up well in the class and placed more than respectably, especially for a horse that could not stand on his own a half year earlier.

Between classes, Heather and Gunner were invited to the media station to tell their story. The little Paint was a celebrity and everyone was talking about "that miracle horse."

Later that afternoon, they were waiting at the gate again for the showmanship class to be called. Heather had pulled together a very good-looking show outfit, minus some glitter, but at a fraction of the money that she would normally have spent. Both she and Gunner were groomed to perfection, and Brent was feeling very proud of the effort he had put in to help get them there. They were just minutes away from the class he'd been waiting for, along with the dozens of other fans who filled the stands that afternoon to get a look at Gunner.

Wes, with Tramp at his heels, was never far from the action, and he stood now, munching a chocolate bar and watching his mother smooth her hair and brush dust from her dress shirt. Gunner chewed on his lead rope, trying to pull it from Brent's hands.

"Do you think Gunner's glad to be here again, Mama?" Wes asked thoughtfully.

Heather rubbed one of Gunner's ears and answered, "Yes, I think he is. He likes all this attention, and he hasn't been this playful in a long time."

Wes reached up and offered Gunner the last of his Snickers bar, and before Heather or Brent could stop him, Gunner was munching the half-melted, gooey

treat, tossing his head and flicking bits of chocolaty saliva when the candy stuck to his teeth. Wes laid his hands on either side of the gelding's white face and kissed him.

"I'm glad you're still here," he whispered.

It was a sweet and moving moment, but Brent and Heather exchanged looks of dismay when Gunner raised his head again. Chocolate smudges marred the perfect white face that they had labored so hard to make gleaming. A year ago, this would have been a disaster and sent Heather into a tailspin. Now, she looked from Brent's shocked expression to her son's broad smile to Gunner's chocolate muzzle, and she burst out laughing. With minutes to spare, they cleaned the chocolate off as best they could, and Heather and Gunner hurried into the ring to join the rest of the competitors.

Gunner conducted himself like a pro, responding to the tiniest cues, moving with the crisp energy and subtle flare that had earned him top honors the year before. He was underweight and still bore the scars of his hurricane ordeal, and his eye was dark and sightless now, but Brent, watching from the sidelines, saw them dance. It was enough to advance them to the finals in the class, despite all that was against them. He would not be named champion that year, but in Heather's, Wesley's, and Brent's eyes, and to everyone who knew him, he was a champion beyond all measure.

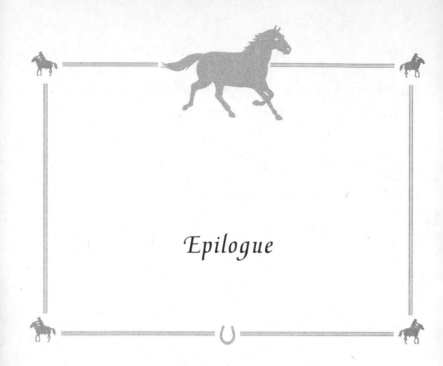

Epilogue

PBJ Decks Smokin Gun still lives with Buttermilk at the little farm in Picayune, Mississippi. Gunner's hardships were not over. The young horse survived a tragic trailer wreck a year after his return to the Worlds – a wreck which took the life of six-year-old Wesley and a young girl who had been traveling home from a show with them. Gunner has been one of the reasons that Heather has been able to find a way forward. He is still sassy and full of life, despite the incredible challenges he has faced, and he remains one of her most beloved friends.

This story is written in memory of
Wesley William Goodwin,
August 2000 – June 2007.

True HORSE Stories by Judy Andrekson:

Little Squire: The Jumping Pony
Miskeen: The Dancing Horse
JB Andrew: Mustang Magic
Fosta: Marathon Master
Brigadier: Gentle Hero
Gunner: Hurricane Horse